THE LITTLE BOOK OF AFRICAN WISDOM

The Little Book of African Wisdom

First published in the UK by
New Internationalist Publications Ltd., Oxford, England.

Compilation © Patrick Ibekwe/New Internationalist 2002.
Reprinted 2004, 2005, 2007, 2009, 2010.

Printed on recycled paper by C&C Offset Printing Co. Ltd., China.
Designed by Alan Hughes.

British Library Cataloguing-in-Publication Data.
A catalogue record for this book is available from the British Library.

ISBN 978-1-906523-20-6

New Internationalist Publications Ltd.
Registered Office: 55 Rectory Road, Oxford OX4 1BW.

www.newint.org

THE LITTLE BOOK OF
AFRICAN
WISDOM

Compiled by **Patrick Ibekwe**

New Internationalist

Patrick Ibekwe lives in London, and follows closely political and social developments in Nigeria, his family's country of origin.

Foreword

I have long been interested in and derived a great deal of pleasure from reading proverbial and aphoristic literature, with its fascinating combination of pith and point. The difference between the two forms is essentially one of provenance. Proverbs and aphorisms may be described as terse, general statements, often using figurative language, touching upon some aspect of life. But whereas the originators of aphorisms are invariably known Westerners, such as Samuel Johnson or Emerson, a proverb is a traditional saying, origin unknown, which has been handed down from generation to generation as a common inheritance.

A collection of African proverbs, it seemed to me, ought to encompass as many of the myriad cultures of that continent as possible; and while it would probably be impossible to include proverbs from every one of the hundreds of cultural and linguistic traditions that flourish across the continent, it certainly ought to be possible to cover most of the major peoples.

Taking 'African' to include anyone of African descent, wherever they happen to be in the world, it seemed to me that the project could and ought to be broadened to take in diaspora culture. And so my work of collecting proverbs assumed its final form: proverbs traversing Africa, the Caribbean and the Americas.

Patrick Ibekwe
London

'Tis better to give

*G*iving is a matter of the heart, don't say it is a matter of wealth.

SWAHILI (EAST AFRICA)

*B*etter the smallest present than the most magnificent meanness.

HAUSA (NIGER and NIGERIA)

*G*iving hands receive.

UGANDAN

Persevere!

Rest cannot shorten the way; going ahead does.

TSONGA (MOZAMBIQUE)

Fe walk fi nuttin better dan fe si' down fe nuttin.

JAMAICAN

To walk for nothing is better than to sit down for nothing.

Adaptability

*W*hen thrown into the sea the stone
said, 'After all, this is also a home.'
UGANDAN

Greedy guts

Do not run after a hen with salt in your hand.
THONGA (ZIMBABWE and SOUTH AFRICA)

Do not drink water in the house of a merchant: he will charge you for it.
ANCIENT EGYPTIAN

She who wants all, tells the rest to be contented.

UGANDAN

Business is business

A gift is a gift, and a purchase is a purchase; so no one will thank you for saying 'I sold it you very cheap.'
YORUBA (BENIN, NIGERIA and TOGO)

Caution...

The grasshopper that sleeps forgetfully wakes up in the mouth of the lizard.
IGBO (NIGERIA)

The wound we took care of has healed.
OVAMBO (ANGOLA and NAMIBIA)

...and carelessness

If you have no time to take care of your sickness, you get time to die.
TSHI (GHANA)

Wealth

Let an orphan get rich and she will find relatives.

UGANDAN

Wealth takes charge of its owner.

ANCIENT EGYPTIAN

Where there is no wealth, there is no poverty.

TSWANA (BOTSWANA and SOUTH AFRICA)

Take it easy

Don't hurry to love someone. Perhaps she hates you. Don't hurry to hate her. Perhaps she loves you.

FULFULDE (WEST AFRICA)

There's the rub

Two buttocks cannot avoid friction.
TONGA (ZAMBIA)

When men fight by the light of the moon, the bald ones are sure to be hit.

MALAGASY (MADAGASCAR)

True colours

As soon as the monkey has climbed a tree, it will start abusing you from its elevated position.

NAMIBIAN

She who gave to me is the same as she who withheld from you.

SWAHILI (EAST AFRICA)

The tree fell the way it leant.

FIPA (TANZANIA)

Don't fight it

Accept the weather as it comes and people as they are.

HAITIAN

The peacemaker

'Stop! Let the quarrel come to an end': so says one whose friend is winning.

GANDA (UGANDA)

Appreciation

Bring me flowers while I am still alive.
SWAHILI (EAST AFRICA)

The rainbow might be better lookin' if 'twasn't such a cheap show.
AFRICAN-AMERICAN

Those who wear pearls do not know how often the shark bites the leg of the diver.
AMHARIC (ETHIOPIA)

Risk assessment

When two deer are fighting and they see a lion, they run off together.
TSHI (GHANA)

The person who knows the ford well is the one whom the crocodile seizes.
HAUSA (NIGER and NIGERIA)

Desire

*D*esires tie.

KIKUYU (KENYA)

*W*here the heart longs to be the path never reaches.
SHONA (MOZAMBIQUE and ZIMBABWE)

Family ties

Impatience with your
brother is in the flesh,
it doesn't reach the bone.
**MAMPRUSSI
(BURKINA FASO)**

Mother carry me, I
too will carry you.
**BEMBA
(D R CONGO, ZAMBIA and
ZIMBABWE)**

Stay focused

The person who pursues two rats will miss both.

YORUBA (BENIN, NIGERIA and TOGO)

Two-faced

The teeth that laugh are also those that bite.
HAUSA (NIGER and NIGERIA)

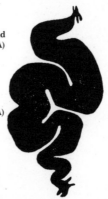

To be smiled at is not to be loved.
KIKUYU (KENYA)

If they are praising your climbing skill, they are also predicting your fall.
EWE (GHANA, BENIN and TOGO)

Think it over

A heart that does not reflect will speak a thoughtless word.
GANDA (UGANDA)

C hew until it is soft before you swallow.
LUYIA (KENYA and UGANDA)

Anger

The greatest remedy for anger is delay.
SWAHILI (EAST AFRICA)

It is better to spend the night in anger
than in repentance.
TAMASHEK (ALGERIA, MALI and NIGER)

Traitor!

I do not mind the one who catches me
but she who gives me away.

KIKUYU (KENYA)

The finger of blame

*W*hen a clean person pollutes the air, people often blame the dirty person in their midst.

LUYIA (KENYA and UGANDA)

*W*hether it was the tenant who seduced the landlord's wife, or the landlord who seduced the tenant's wife, it is the tenant who would leave the house.

IGBO (NIGERIAN)

The choice is yours

If the river prevents crossing, it will not prevent turning back.

HAUSA (NIGER and NIGERIA)

Bringing up baby

A tree is straightened when it is young.
OVAMBO (ANGOLA and NAMIBIA)

A bsence does not raise a child.
TSHI (GHANA)

W hatever the parents talk at midnight, the children talk at midday.
OROMO (ETHIOPIA and KENYA)

The full flush of youth

The young bull mounts the cows from the head.

KIKUYU (KENYA)

Elders see and keep silent, but to see and talk are signs of the young.

IGBO (NIGERIA)

Old age

Grow old, body, the heart still remains.
NDEBELE (ZIMBABWE)

You can run away from your elder, but she'll outthink you.
SUKUMA (TANZANIA)

Fear

When fear enters, truth escapes.
SWAHILI (EAST AFRICA)

Through thick and thin

*O*ne who is
quick to act
in your favour is a
real friend.
HAYA (TANZANIA)

*P*romise get
frien';
perform keep am.
GUYANAN

*Promise gets a friend;
performance keeps him.*

*T*oo much love spoils the friendship.
KIKUYU (KENYA)

Sworn enemies

People who fight on the ground should not go up the tree together.
OROMO (ETHIOPIA and KENYA)

Rising early to greet an enemy is a poor game.
HAUSA (NIGER and NIGERIA)

The worm don't see nothing pretty in the robin's song.
AFRICAN-AMERICAN

Praise be

*D*o not blame God for having created
the tiger, but thank Him for not
having given it wings.

AMHARIC (ETHIOPIA)

Limits

Leaps and bounds and measured paces all end at the seashore.

TSHI (GHANA)

Every river that runs into the sea loses its name.

TSHI (GHANA)

Not impressed

The eyes which have seen the
mountains are not moved by valleys.
SWAHILI (EAST AFRICA)

Guilty conscience

Guilt never decays.
SOTHO (BOTSWANA, LESOTHO and SOUTH AFRICA)

It's because the rat knows what he does at night that he doesn't go out during the day.

HAITIAN

A clear conscience is a soft mat.
SWAHILI (EAST AFRICA)

There's gratitude for you

*D*o a man a favour and he'll never forgive you.

HAITIAN

*Y*ou have cured his testicles, and he has used them on your wife.

UGANDAN

*P*eople count the refusals, [they] do not count the gifts.

KIKUYU (KENYA)

Quality not quantity

The depth of a person's life is more important than its length.

SWAHILI (EAST AFRICA)

Good manners don't hurt

If you no got smile on you face, no use open shop.

JAMAICAN

Good manners is civilization.
SWAHILI (EAST AFRICA)

If you visit the village of the toads and you find them squatting, you must squat too.
EWE (GHANA, BENIN and TOGO)

Matters of the heart

A cough and love cannot be hidden.
TSONGA (MOZAMBIQUE)

I f you want to hear news of the heart, ask the face.

FULANI (WEST AFRICA)

L ove is a cover: it hides all shortcomings.
SHONA (MOZAMBIQUE and ZIMBABWE)

Chalk and cheese

The penis does not know what the vagina thinks.

IGBO (NIGERIA)

Disappointment

Fire gives birth to ashes.

SUKUMA (TANZANIA)

Commonsense...

Common sense born before book.
BAJAN (BARBADOS)

...and learning

He who does not ask a question learns nothing.
SWAHILI (EAST AFRICA)

Wealth, if you use it, comes to an end; learning, if you use it, increases.
SWAHILI (EAST AFRICA)

The voice of experience

'Let-it-cool-down' had already burnt itself.

SHONA (MOZAMBIQUE and ZIMBABWE)

New broom sweep clean, but de ole [old] broom know de carner [corner].

JAMAICAN

Taken to extremes

Exaggerated love brings exaggerated hatred.

OROMO (ETHIOPIA and KENYA)

If one person eats all the honey, he is sure to get a belly-ache.

TSHI (GHANA)

We do not cut open someone's head to see what is in it.

TSHI (GHANA)

Ability

*D*o not hurl a lance if you cannot control its aim.

ANCIENT EGYPTIAN

*T*hat which pecks on a rock should have a tough beak.

LUYIA (KENYA and ETHIOPIA)

The feeling is mutual

You are afraid of a snake and it is afraid of you.

OVAMBO (ANGOLA and NAMIBIA)

Appearances

A silk dress doesn't mean clean under-garments.

HAITIAN

As one's appearance so they give seat.

IGBO (NIGERIA)

The overdraft

A s always, the loaned pot got broken.

UGANDAN

Rubbing off

W hen you sleep wid darg [dog] you ketch [catch] him flea.

JAMAICAN

Braveheart and yellow belly

We risk death and find safety.

JABO (LIBERIA)

A cowardly hyena lives longer.

TONGA (ZAMBIA)

General Coward and General Prudence are two different persons.

HAITIAN

Forgetting

The tongue forgets more than the ear.
UGANDAN

To forget is the same as to throw away.
AFRICAN

Drunk and tedious

When de rum a in, de wit a out.

JAMAICAN

When the rum is in, the wit is out.

Gatecrashers

If you invite yourself, bring your own chair.

SWAHILI (EAST AFRICA)

Force of habit

Habit is a full-grown mountain, hard to get over or to pull down.
                    **KONGO (ANGOLA, CONGO
                    AND D R CONGO)**

Happiness

*H*appiness requires something to do, something to love and something to hope for.

SWAHILI (EAST AFRICA)

*S*he who sows joy harvests pleasure.

HAITIAN

Blissful ignorance?

Ignorance caused the chicken to sleep hungry on top of the bundle of corn.
HAUSA (NIGER and NIGERIA)

Not to know is bad, not to wish to know is worse.
WOLOF (GAMBIA and SENEGAL)

Ways of going about it

Long road draw sweat, short cut draw blood.

JAMAICAN

By the side of 'I shall do' was found 'Not yet done'.

KIKUYU (KENYA)

Go get it

The chakata fruit on the ground belongs to all, but the one on the tree is for she who can climb.

SHONA (MOZAMBIQUE and ZIMBABWE)

Lazy bones

A lazy person does not know they are lazy until they drive a tortoise away and it escapes.

HAUSA (NIGER and NIGERIA)

L aziness and hunger are twins.

SWAHILI (EAST AFRICA)

S itting together won't do the work.

MAMPRUSSI (BURKINA FASO)

T he lazy person who goes to borrow a spade says, 'I hope I won't find one!'

MALAGASY (MADAGASCAR)

Tying the knot

The man who says he will not marry a woman with other admirers, will not marry a woman.

YORUBA (BENIN, NIGERIA and TOGO)

The way you got married is not the way you'll get divorced.

HAITIAN

Courtship is not marriage.

UGANDAN

Lonely heart

The woods are not heartless (ie there is comfort in solitude).

SOUTHERN AFRICA

Filthy lucre

Money is not counted well for you by somebody else.

GANDA (UGANDA)

The size of your purse is the measure of your charm.

HAITIAN

Food can be refused after I have had my fill but not money.

SHONA (MOZAMBIQUE and ZIMBABWE)

Poverty

A house of nothing but mud: the conflagration turns away in shame.

HAUSA (NIGER and NIGERIA)

Poor people entertain with the heart.

HAITIAN

Poverty is like a lion, if you do not fight you get eaten.

HAYA (TANZANIA)

The monkey says that there is nothing like poverty for taking the conceit out of a man.

ASHANTI (GHANA)

Obsession

To look too hard is to become blind.

FIPA (TANZANIA)

Get your priorities straight

I fried the oil and forgot the onion.
HAUSA (NIGER and NIGERIA)

One whose house is on fire never hunts the rats running from it.
IGBO (NIGERIA)

The green-eyed monster

The eyes which you cure will one day look at you with envy.
LUO (KENYA and TANZANIA)

A stone will sooner soften than jealousy.
TSWANA (BOTSWANA and SOUTH AFRICA)

Lies, damned lies

Lies return.

KAONDE (ZAMBIA)

If you sow falsehood, you reap deceit.

AFRICAN

Liars should have good memories.

SWAHILI (EAST AFRICA)

The whiff of scandal

Scandal is like an egg: when it is hatched it has wings.

MALAGASY (MADAGASCAR)

A hog that has wallowed in the mud seeks a clean person to rub against.

YORUBA (BENIN, NIGERIA and TOGO)

Promises

A promise is a debt.

SWAHILI (EAST AFRICA)

You and nobody else

In doing good one does it to oneself; in doing evil one does it to oneself.

TAMASHEK (ALGERIA, MALI and NIGER)

Thirst cannot be quenched by proxy.

MONGO (D R CONGO)

Memory

*D*o not observe what is before and forget what is behind.

SWAHILI (EAST AFRICA)

*M*emory reaches further than the eyes.

KANURI (CHAD, NIGER and NIGERIA)

War...

War begets no good offspring.
MONGO (D R CONGO)

De [the] soldier's blood, de general's name.

JAMAICAN

...and peace

It is better to build bridges than walls.
SWAHILI (EAST AFRICA)

Remedies

The medicine for hate is separation.
FULFULDE (WEST AFRICA)

To forget a wrong is the best revenge.
SWAHILI (EAST AFRICA)

Pulling rank

A s one's rank, so they give seat.
IGBO (NIGERIA)

K ings may grow
beards as they do
not have to blow the
fire.

NIGERIAN

Lack

*D*e want of a thing is more dan de wort'.

JAMAICAN

The want of a thing is more than the worth.

A good name

A good name shines in the dark.
SWAHILI (EAST AFRICA)

Do not handle mud when there is no water.
SHONA (MOZAMBIQUE and ZIMBABWE)

Leave a good name behind in case you return.
GOGO (TANZANIA)

Fools rush in

*W*hat is built on chance is built on sand.

HAITIAN

Shoulder to the wheel

No sweet without sweat. **UGANDAN**

Riches are like perspiration: if you rest, they dry up.

GANDA (UGANDA)

Fair shares

'Ours' is not 'mine'. SWAHILI (EAST AFRICA)

People who share with others are seldom hungry.

HAITIAN

Put it down, let us divide it; things fought over get spoilt.

LAMBA (D R CONGO and ZAMBIA)

Be prepared

Left hand, learn before the right one is broken.

OVAMBO (ANGOLA and NAMIBIA)

One does not make a shield on the battlefield.

AFRICAN

Pride

'I have taken a shortcut,' says she who has gone astray.

UGANDAN

May the force be with you

P r'yer in de mout' only is no pr'yer.

JAMAICAN

Prayer in the mouth only is no prayer.

P r'yer needn't be long when fait'[h] [s]'trong.

JAMAICAN

'G od help me!': you have a right to pray so if you also exert yourself.

GANDA (UGANDA)

Mistakes...

To lose your way is one way of finding it.

SWAHILI (EAST AFRICA)

...and repentance

Repentance is deeds.

SWAHILI (EAST AFRICA)

Tit-for-tat

He who sells sand as salt will get stone as money.
YORUBA (BENIN, NIGERIA and TOGO)

If you consider your friend to be an animal he considers you to be shit.
TSHI (GHANA)

What comes naturally

*P*uss may look 'pon king, but him rader ratta.

JAMAICAN

A cat may look upon a king, but he would rather look upon a rat.

*T*he gazelle jumps, and should her child crawl?

FULFULDE (WEST AFRICA)

Colonialism

If there had been no poverty in Europe, then the white man would not have come and spread his clothes in Africa.

TSHI (GHANA)

Ulterior motives

The vulture does not circle without reason.

KAMBA (KENYA and TANZANIA)

Luck of the draw

The lucky eagle kills a mouse that has eaten salt.

UGANDAN

When you're unlucky, a potato peel can cut your foot.

HAITIAN

If need be

A panting animal will stop under
any tree.

KIKUYU (KENYA)

S he who has necessity has no shame.

KIKUYU (KENYA)

H e who wants what is under the bed
must stoop for it.

SWAHILI (EAST AFRICA)

Bear your burden

One should not invite a curse and leave it to another to bear.

TWI (GHANA)

You blame the wolf even though the goats are wandering in the meadow at night.

OVAMBO (ANGOLA and NAMIBIA)

Self-help

A mouth does not eat on behalf of another.
SHONA (MOZAMBIQUE and ZIMBABWE)

It is no good asking the spirits to help you run if you don't mean to sprint.
GANDA (UGANDA)

No regrets

Doing one's best drives away regret.
MALAGASY (MADAGASCAR)

It is better to spend the night in the irritation of the offence than in repentance for the revenge.
TAMASHEK (ALGERIA, MALI, NIGERIA)

The emperor's new clothes

Everyone's character is good in their own eyes.
YORUBA (BENIN, NIGERIA and TOGO)

The king's dog thinks that they bow to it because of its bark.
UGANDAN

Spot the likeness

Anyone with an anus will not laugh at
another's fart.
OVAMBO (ANGOLA and NAMIBIA)

There is no difference between a thief
and his accomplice.
KIKUYU (KENYA)

Here comes trouble

Trouble an' sea no gat no back doo'.
GUYANAN

Trouble and the sea have got no back door.

Trouble mek puss run up prickly pear.
JAMAICAN

Trouble makes the cat run up the prickly pear tree.

Yikes

The swearing is out of proportion to what is lost; a needle is lost and an oath is taken upon a god!

YORUBA (BENIN, NIGERIA and TOGO)

Questions

A question is not an accusation.
GANDA (UGANDA)

If a matter be dark, dive to the bottom.
YORUBA (BENIN, NIGERIA and TOGO)

Had enough!

She who is sated spits out honey.
GALLA (KENYA and ETHIOPIA)

When the cat's belly is full, he says that the rat's tail is bitter.
HAITIAN

Variety's spice

A man who eats what he has, his desire is for what he has not.

IGBO (NIGERIA)

Why worry

If it has not happened to you, sleep.

TSHI (GHANA)

Temptation and sin

Debil a-tempt, but he no a-fo'ce.
GUYANAN

The devil tempts, but he doesn't force.

Sin devours the one who has committed it.
SHONA (MOZAMBIQUE and ZIMBABWE)

Wrongdoing is a hill: you walk on your own and observe that of another.
HAUSA (NIGER and NIGERIA)

Self, self, self

Let my cow die here rather than give birth at your place.

UGANDAN

When I find hard work to do, I call my friends to help me; but when I find a well-salted eel, I find I don't need help.

MALAGASY (MADAGASCAR)

New horizons

The traveller can tell all she has seen on her journey, but she can't explain it all.

TSHI (GHANA)

Travelling means finding.

UGANDAN

To each their own

The great are open to shame, and the small are open to fear.

MALAGASY (MADAGASCAR)

Speech

A word fallen on the ground [ie spoken] is left to be picked up by others.

KIKUYU (KENYA)

F ish get ketch by e mout'.

CREOLE (BELIZE)

The fish gets caught by his mouth.

C onversation is the food of the ears.

TRINIDADIAN

Silence

_S_ till tongue keep wise head.

GUYANAN

_T_ he eyes are for seeing, the ears for hearing, and the lips to shut up.

HAITIAN

_T_ o know and keep quiet is wickedness.

MAMPRUSSI (BURKINA FASO)

No ifs and buts

When you see ole lady run, no ax wha'de matter, run too.

JAMAICAN

When you see the old lady run, don't ask what's the matter, run too.

Unity

Pig and mud go together.
SHONA (MOZAMBIQUE and ZIMBABWE)

People often agree in words but not in judgement.
KIKUYU (KENYA)

Two people in accord are stronger than eight who disagree.
SWAHILI (EAST AFRICA)

Sympathy

Sympathy doesn't cure a sore.

TSHI (GHANA)

If you know what hurts yourself you know what hurts others.

MALAGASY (MADAGASCAR)

The world within

A person's thoughts are their kingdom.
TSONGA (MOZAMBIQUE)

Willing to help

A de willin' harse dem saddle mos'.

JAMAICAN

It's the willing horse they saddle most.

T he volunteer is worth ten pressed men.

HAUSA (NIGER and NIGERIA)

Be prepared

*W*hat is not sharpened does not cut.
SWAHILI (EAST AFRICA)

Death

At someone's funeral we weep for our own mothers and fathers.

TSHI (GHANA)

At the funeral, one cries for the living and not for the dead.

IGBO (NIGERIA)

The way it goes

*W*hat you push away from you today with your foot, you will pick up tomorrow with your hand.

MARTINIQUE

Truth

One who tells the truth makes no mistakes.

SWAHILI (EAST AFRICA)

Telling the truth can dig a grave.

SURINAMESE

Gilded words

A multitude of words cloaks a lie.

HAUSA (NIGER and NIGERIA)

People in glass houses

Y ou cannot point an accusing finger without leaving four directed at yourself.

IGBO (NIGERIA)

M y eyes, look at me too.
OVAMBO (ANGOLA and NAMIBIA)

Simple solutions

*D*arg [dog] no howl if him hab [have] bone.

JAMAICAN

'*D*on't do it' is the best remedy for 'let it not be known'.

NUPE (NIGERIA)

Use and worth

Dutty [dirty] water wi'[ll] put out fire.

JAMAICAN

If one could not make use of gold dust,
then it would merely be called sand.

ASHANTI (GHANA)

Taking care of number one

A horse brings you to the battlefield,
but it does not fight.

GURAGE (ETHIOPIA)

E ach firefly lights its own way.

HAITIAN

Remember you had help

Those who have succeeded forget
those who have helped them succeed.
GANDA (UGANDA)

Hope

Hope is the pillar of the world.
KANURI (CHAD, NIGER and NIGERIA)

Discreet advice

Dirty clothes are washed in the backyard.

SWAHILI (EAST AFRICA)

Rabbit says, 'Drink everything, eat everything, but don't tell everything.'

MARTINIQUE

Injury

It is not difficult to hurt, but it is difficult to repair.

TSONGA (MOZAMBIQUE)

A scar is easily wounded.

SWAHILI (EAST AFRICA)

Human nature

In the midst of your illness you will promise a goat, but when you have recovered, a chicken will seem sufficient.
JUKUN (NIGERIA)

If you were medicine you would be very bitter.

EFIK (NIGERIA)

Other people

It is not necessary to blow out the other person's lantern to let yours shine.

SWAHILI (EAST AFRICA)

We are people because of other people.

SOTHO (BOTSWANA, LESOTHO and SOUTH AFRICA)

When it is not your mother who is in danger of being eaten by the wild animal, the matter can wait until tomorrow.

GANDA (UGANDA)

Weak and wayward

A weak person goes where he is smiled at.

HERERO (NAMIBIA)

A re you a flag – to follow every breeze?

SWAHILI (EAST AFRICA)

The best policy?

Too long honest, too long poor.

BAJAN (BARBADOS)

Dishonour

Hell itself holds dishonour in horror.

TAMASHEK (ALGERIA, MALI and NIGER)

Unhealthy development

*O*ver-discipline makes a child stunted.
IGBO (NIGERIA)

*I*f you are given bread for foolishness,
you may despise instruction.
ANCIENT EGYPTIAN

Hot gossip

The tongue carries that which is light.

TSHI (GHANA)

Forgiveness

Forgiving is victory.

SWAHILI (EAST AFRICA)

If you do not forgive a crime, you commit a crime.

TWI (GHANA)

Duh!

A self-made fool is worse than a natural one.

KIKUYU (KENYA)

O nly fool put puss [cat] fe [to] watch milk.

JAMAICAN

Hunger...

A hungry stomach knows no law.
TSONGA (MOZAMBIQUE)

Hunger will make a monkey eat pepper.
HAITIAN

..and eating

There is no god like the throat: it takes sacrifices daily.
NIGERIAN

Rock bottom

The hen of a poor person does not lay eggs, and even if she lays eggs, she never hatches, and if she hatches, she never rears the chicks, and when she rears, the chicks are taken by the hawk.

SWAHILI (EAST AFRICA)

Join hands

The hand of the child cannot reach the shelf, nor [can] the hand of the adult get through the neck of the gourd.

YORUBA (BENIN, NIGERIA and TOGO)

One hand must wash the other.

TSWANA (BOTSWANA and SOUTH AFRICA)

Common courtesy

Politeness costs so little and is worth so much.

HAITIAN

It is a mere formality for a small bird to invite an elephant in to its nest.

SHONA (MOZAMBIQUE and ZIMBABWE)

Object lessons

Examples have children.

TSHI (GHANA)

Favours enslave.

SWAHILI (EAST AFRICA)

Do the right thing

*C*hoose your fellow traveller before you start on your journey.
HAUSA (NIGER and NIGERIA)

*U*se your clay while it is wet.
SWAHILI (EAST AFRICA)

Followers

No one who is following an elephant
has to knock the dew off the grass.
ASHANTI (GHANA)

Follow-fashion bruk [broke] monkey
neck.
JAMAICAN

Access all areas

L ove enters even though it is forbidden.
THONGA (ZIMBABWE and SOUTH AFRICA)

Childcare

The chicken with children doesn't swallow the worm.

SUKUMA (TANZANIA)

A perverse streak

When you gave him he refused, but when you placed it back he stole and finished it.

OROMO (ETHIOPIA and KENYA)

Perspectives

It is playing for children and [an] emergency for the butterfly.
OROMO (ETHIOPIA and KENYA)

Hog run for him life; dog run for him character.

BAHAMIAN

Humble beginnings

A little path can lead far away.

HAITIAN

A spark burns down the forest.

OVAMBO (ANGOLA and NAMIBIA)

What is tried may become true.

OVAMBO (ANGOLA and NAMIBIA)

DIY

'Save me' is a slow deliverance; help
yourself.
TSWANA (BOTSWANA and SOUTH AFRICA)

All too soon

The night is over before one has finished counting the stars!

FIPA (TANZANIA)

Advice

Advice is like mushrooms: you pick what you like.
SHONA (MOZAMBIQUE and ZIMBABWE)

And, finally...

When the occasion comes, the proverb comes.

OJI (GHANA)